active minds

numbers

PHOTOGRAPHY

George Siede and Donna Preis

CONSULTANT

Istar Schwager, Ph.D.

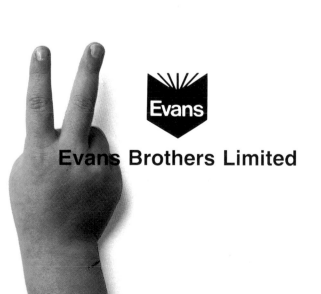

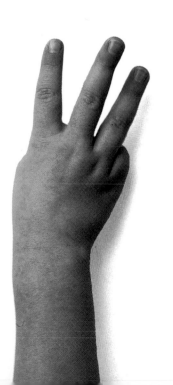

Evans

Evans Brothers Limited

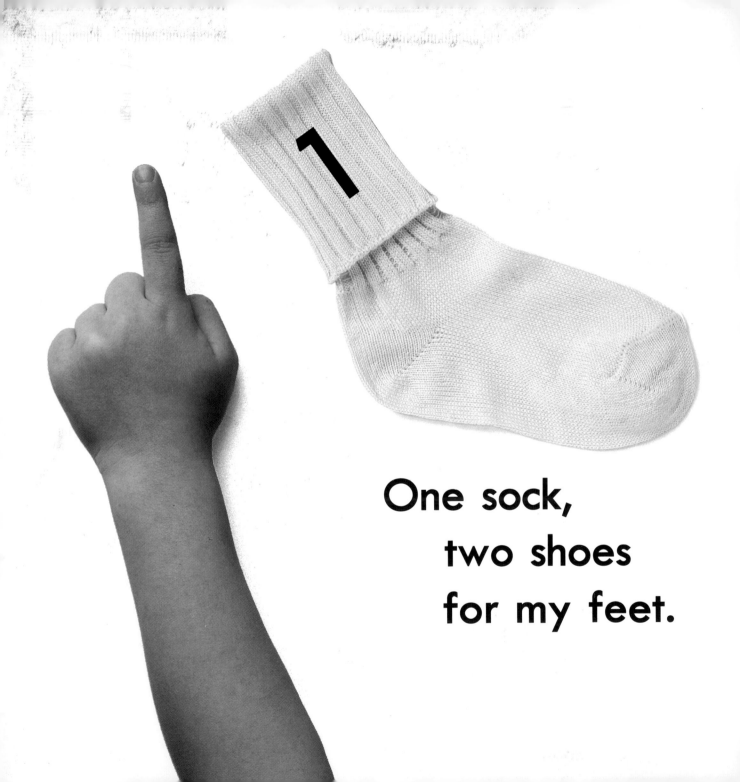

One sock,
two shoes
for my feet.

Consultant Istar Schwager holds a PhD in educational psychology
and a master's degree in early childhood education.
She has been an advisor for numerous child development and early learning programmes,
including the television programme Sesame Street, and has regularly written articles for parents on a range of topics.

C 1992 Publications International Ltd

First published in Great Britain in 1993 by
Evans Brothers Ltd
2A Portman Mansions
Chiltern Street
London W1M 1LE

Printed in Slovenia by DELO - Tiskarna, Ljubljana

ISBN 0 237 51318 8

Three, then

four

good things to eat.

1

2

Five balloons

up in the sky.

1 2 3

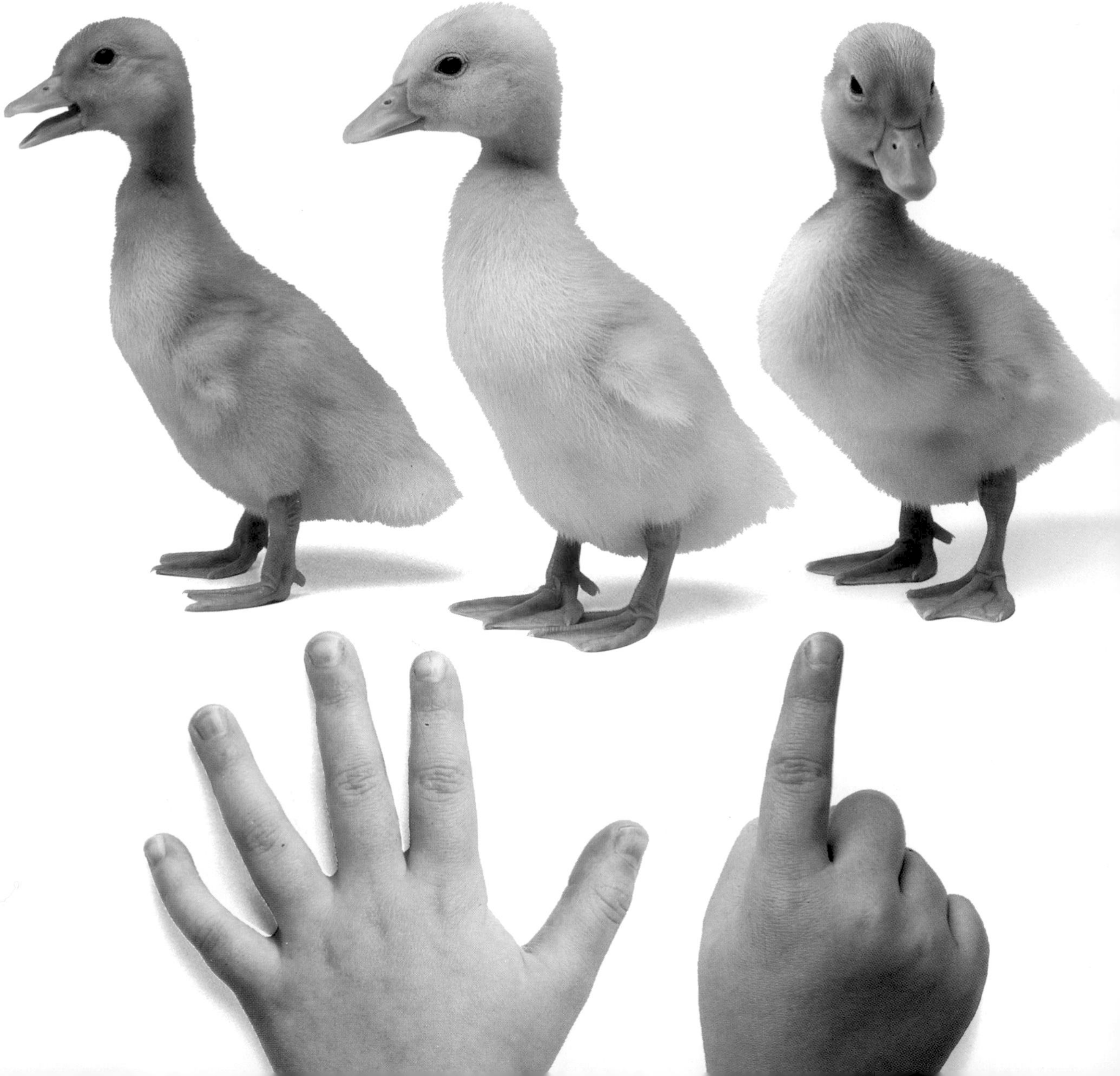

4

5

6

Six ducklings walking by.

Seven flowers
standing tall.

5 6 7 8

Eight puppies with a ball.

Nine melons,
juicy and red.

Ten animals
for my bed.